reading level- 2.8
A.R. Pts. - .5   820L   · 2009

D1524682

Wrinkles, Warts & Wattles

Lynn M. Stone

Rourke
Publishing LLC
Vero Beach, Florida 32964

www.rourkepublishing.com

PHOTO CREDITS: cover © Lynn Stone: title page, 5, 6, 7, 8, 9, 11, 13, 14, 15, 17, 18, 19, 20, 21; ©Josh Webb: page 4; © Nico Smit: page 10; © Carolina Garcia Aranda: page 12; © Mepp: page 16;

Editor: Meg Greve

Cover design by: Nicola Stratford, bdpublishing.com

Interior design by: Renee Brady

Library of Congress Cataloging-in-Publication Data

Stone, Lynn M.

Wrinkles, warts, and wattles : / Lynn M. Stone.
   p. cm. -- (What animals wear)
 Includes index.
 ISBN 978-1-60472-312-0 (hardcover)
 ISBN 978-1-60472-790-6 (softcover)
 1. Skin--Juvenile literature. 2. Body covering (Anatomy)--Juvenile
literature. I. Title.
 QL941S86 2009
 591.47--dc22
                          2008012972

Printed in the USA

CG/CG

Table of Contents

 Wrinkles

Loose, wrinkly skin is good for an elephant. Loose skin means more skin. More skin helps release more heat.

Elephants live in warm places where baggy skin helps them stay cool.

Several kinds of dogs have **wrinkles**. Dog breeders developed wrinkly dogs just for show.

The **basset hound** is well known for its wrinkles.

Warts

Tiny germs called viruses cause real warts. However, many animals have lumps that look like warts.

The warts on a **warthog** are really lumps of skin and hard tissue called cartilage.

The warthog's warts may help protect its eyes in fights. The toad's warty skin can ooze liquid that hurts other animals.

Touching
a toad
does not
cause warts!

Wattles

Many kinds of birds have **wattles**. Wattles are globs, strings, or lumps of fatty flesh. Wattles usually hang from a bird's cheeks or neck.

The ground hornbill has wattles on its neck and around its eyes.

Wattles help birds show off during courtship. The wattles on a wattled **crane** become brighter when seeking a mate.

The tom turkey's wattle helps it attract a mate.

Courtship leads to nesting and raising babies. The survival of any animal depends upon raising babies.

Roosters are the most common birds with wattles.

Wattles help birds signal changes in their mood. A change in mood changes the color of the wattle on a **cassowary**.

The cassowary is one of the Earth's rarest and oldest kinds of birds.

An animal's wrinkles, warts, or wattles might look funny, but they help the animal stay alive!

The hornbill can fill its wattle with air to make a loud noise.

Glossary

 **basset hound** (BAS-et HOUND): a type of hound dog with short legs and long ears

 **cassowary** (KA-suh-wayr-ee): a tall, flightless bird of Australia and New Guinea

 **crane** (KRANE): a tall, long-legged bird that lives in meadows and marshes

warthog (WORT-hog): a type of wild African pig

wattles (WOT-uhlz): meaty pieces of flesh on the cheeks or necks of certain animals

wrinkles (RING-huhls): folds in the skin

Index

Further Reading

Arnosky, Jim. *All About Turkeys*. Scholastic, 2008.

Holmes, Kevin. *Warthogs*. Coughlan, 1999.

Kalman, Bobbie. *Endangered Elephants*. Crabtree, 2005.

Websites

www.enchantedlearning.com'subjects'birds'label'turkey'index.shtml

www.nationalgeographic.com'kids'creature_feature/0106/warthogs.html

www.surfnetkids.com/elephant.htm

About the Author

   Lynn M. Stone is a widely-published wildlife and domestic animal photographer and the author of more than 500 children's books. His book *Box Turtles* was chosen as an Outstanding Science Trade Book and Selectors' Choice for 2008 by the Science Committee of the National Science Teachers' Association and the Children's Book Council.